Wild Animals

ELEPHANT

 Lionel Bender

Chrysalis Children's Books

First published in the UK in 2004 by
Chrysalis Children's Books
An imprint of Chrysalis Books Group Plc,
The Chrysalis Building, Bramley Road,
London W10 6SP

ISBN 1 84458 172 1

British Library Cataloguing in Publication Data
for this book is available from the British Library.

Editorial Manager *Joyce Bentley*
Senior Editor *Rasha Elsaeed*
Editorial Assistant *Camilla Lloyd*

Produced by Bender Richardson White
Project Editor *Lionel Bender*
Designer *Ben White*
Production *Kim Richardson*
Picture Researcher *Cathy Stastny*
Cover Make-up *Mike Pilley, Radius*

Printed in China

10 9 8 7 6 5 4 3 2 1

Words in **Bold** can be found in New words on page 31.

Typography *Natascha Frensch*
Read Regular, READ SMALLCAPS and Read Space; European Community Design Registration 2003
and Copyright © Natascha Frensch 2001-2004 Read Medium, **Read Black** and *Read Slanted*
Copyright © Natascha Frensch 2003-2004

READ™ is a revolutionary new typeface that will enchance children's understanding through clear, easily
recognisable character shapes. With its evenly spaced and carefully designed characters, READ™ will help
children at all stages to improve their literacy skills, and is ideal for young readers, reluctant readers and
especially children with dyslexia.

Picture credits

Cover © Digital Vision. © Digital Vision pages 1, 2, 4, 6, 9, 10, 11, 12, 15, 16, 17, 18, 19, 20, 23, 24, 25. © Corbis Images Inc.:
pages 13 (Peter Johnson), 22 (Corbis), 27 (Anthony Bannister/Gallo Images). © Frank Lane Picture Agency Limited: pages 5
(E. & O. Hosking), 7 (Adriane Van Zandbergen), 8 (Jurgen & Christine Sohns), 14 (Fritz Polking), 21 (F. Lanting/Minden Pictures),
29 (David Hosking). © RSPCA Photolibrary: pages 26 (Nick Greaves), 28 (Klaus-Peter Wolf).

Contents

Elephants 4

Homes 6

Food 8

Big families 10

Daily life 12

Senses 14

Defences 16

Elephant skin 18

Baby elephants 20

Growing up 22

Becoming an adult 24

In danger 26

Elephant care 28

Quiz 30

New words 31

Index 32

Elephants

The elephant is the biggest land animal in the world.

African elephants are bigger than Indian elephants and they have bigger ears.

Homes

Most African elephants live on the **grasslands** of Africa. They often bathe in lakes and rivers.

Some African elephants and most Indian elephants live in thick forests.

Food

An elephant's main food is grass.
It also eats leaves, shoots and fruit.

An elephant pulls up food with its **trunk**, then puts the food in its mouth.

Big families

Elephants live in groups called herds. A herd can have many families.

Each family has lots of adult females and their young. Adult male elephants live separately.

Daily life

To keep clean, an elephant bathes. It also throws water and dust over itself.

Elephants drink by sucking water up into their trunks then squirting it into their mouths.

Senses

An elephant has a good **sense** of smell. It uses its trunk to smell and for touch, too.

An elephant has small eyes and does not see well. With its large ears, its hearing is good.

Defences

An elephant has two huge tusks. When in danger, it will defend itself with its tusks.

When a young elephant is
frightened, it hides beneath its
mother. She protects her young.

Elephant skin

An elephant has very thick, **wrinkled** skin.

The skin on an elephant's ears is thin and flat. The elephant flaps its ears to cool its body.

Baby elephants

A baby elephant is called a calf.
The calf stays close to its mother
and the herd.

The baby elephant feeds on its mother's milk for three years.

Growing up

Calves like to play. They will spray water at one another and roll around in mud.

As a calf grows, it learns to look after itself.

Becoming an adult

A calf becomes an **adult** when it is about 10 years old. An elephant may live for 80 years.

An adult male elephant is called
a bull. An adult female elephant is
called a cow.

In danger

Farmers try to stop elephants coming on their land. This can leave elephants without food.

Some people hunt and kill elephants for their tusks. They use them to make **ornaments**.

Elephant care

To help elephants survive, wildlife carers feed babies whose parents have been killed.

Other young elephants are
looked after in wildlife parks,
safe from hunters.

Quiz

1 How many kinds of elephants are there?

2 What is an elephant's favourite food?

3 What do you call a large group of elephants?

4 What does an elephant use its trunk for?

5 What do baby elephants feed on for the first few months?

6 What are adult male and adult female elephants called?

7 What does an elephant use its tusks for?

8 At what age do elephants become adult?

The answers are all in this book!

New words

adult fully grown and able to make babies.

grasslands huge, open areas of grass dotted with trees.

ornaments objects that look nice but have no special use.

sense the way animals find out about their surroundings. Animals have five senses – sight, hearing, smell, taste and touch. The body senses something when it notices it is there.

trunk long tube that is an elephant's nose and upper lip.

wrinkled with many lines, folds and creases.

Index

adults 11, 24, 25

babies and young 11,
    17, 20–21, 28

bathing 6, 12

defences 16–17

drinking 13

ears 5, 15, 19

eyes 15

families 10–11

females 11, 25

food 8–9, 26

forests 7

grasslands 6

growing up 22–23

hearing 15

herds 10, 20

homes 6–7

males 11, 25

mothers 17, 20, 21

senses 14–15

skin 18–19

smell 14

touch 14

trunk 9, 13, 14

tusks 16, 27